★ HOCKEY SUPERSTARS ★

ALEXANDER OVECHKIN

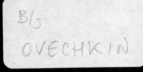

BY SHANE FREDERICK

CAPSTONE PRESS
a capstone imprint

Sports Illustrated Kids Hockey Superstars are published by Capstone Press, 1710 Roe Crest Drive, North Mankato, Minnesota 56003.
www.capstonepub.com

Library of Congress Cataloging-in-Publication Data
Frederick, Shane.
Alexander Ovechkin / by Shane Frederick.
pages cm. – (Sports Illustrated Kids. Hockey Superstars)
Includes bibliographical references and index.
Summary: "Details the life and careeer of hockey superstar Alexander Ovechkin"—Provided by publisher.
Audience: Age: 9-15.
Audience: Grade: 4 to 6.
ISBN 978-1-4914-2141-3 (library binding)
1. Ovechkin, Alexander, 1985—Juvenile literature. 2. Hockey players—Russia (Federation)—Biography—Juvenile literature. I. Title.
GV848.5.O94F74 2015
796.962092—dc23
[B]   2014025989

Editorial Credits
Brenda Haugen, editor; Ted Williams, designer; Eric Gohl, media researcher; Morgan Walters, production specialist

Photo Credits
AP Photo: Paul Connors, 4; Getty Images: Bruce Bennett Studios, 9, 14, Sara Davis, 19; Newscom: Cal Sport Media/Billy Hurst, 10, Icon SMI/IHA, 17, Itar-Tass Photos/Belousov Vitaly, 13; Sports Illustrated: Damian Strohmeyer, 1, David E. Klutho, cover, 16 (inset), 21, 23, 30–31 (background), 32 (background), Robert Beck, 25, Simon Bruty, 7, 26, 29

Design Elements
Shutterstock

Source Note
Page 6, line 7: Associated Press. NHL Gamecenter. 16 Aug. 2001. 14 Aug. 2014.
www.nhl.com/gamecenter/en/recap?id=2005020670

Printed in the United States of America in Stevens Point, Wisconsin.
092014   008479WZS15

TABLE OF CONTENTS

CHAPTER 1

A SCORING SENSATION

Alexander Ovechkin charged down the rink. Only one man remained between him and the goaltender. Just a 20-year-old **rookie**, Ovechkin tried to make a move to get around veteran Phoenix Coyotes player Paul Mara. But the **defenseman** blocked him and knocked him down. Ovechkin slid across the ice and no longer seemed to be a threat to score. But he never lost the puck. With his back to the net and one hand on his stick, he reached over his head. Somehow he shot the puck around the goalie and into the net for a goal!

That play is now known as "The Goal." The highlight has been viewed on YouTube more than 2 million times. Ovechkin has played in the National Hockey League (NHL) for almost a decade, but that goal from his first season continues to amaze fans of all ages.

rookie—a first-year player

defenseman—a player who lines up in a defensive zone to prevent opponents from getting open shots on goal

Wayne Gretzky was the coach of the Coyotes at the time and watched Ovechkin's goal from the bench. No player in NHL history has scored more goals than Gretzky, also known as "The Great One." Even he was impressed with Ovechkin's amazing goal. "That was pretty sweet," Gretzky said.

The Goal is just one of hundreds Ovechkin has scored in his career. Many of those are nearly as electrifying. When he came to the United States from Russia in 2005, the Washington Capitals **winger** quickly became a superstar. He emerged as one of the NHL's all-time great goal scorers, putting up numbers the league hadn't seen in several years.

winger—a type of forward who usually stays near the sides of the zone

FAST FACT

Alexander Ovechkin was the sixth-fastest NHL player to score 400 goals. He did it in 634 games. Only Wayne Gretzky, Mike Bossy, Mario Lemieux, Brett Hull, and Jari Kurri did it in fewer games.

RUSSIA'S YOUNG DYNAMO

Alexander Ovechkin was born September 17, 1985, in Moscow, the capital of Russia. Back then the country was part of a bigger nation called the Soviet Union. The Soviet Union had some of the best hockey players in the world. But in those days, few players left their country for the NHL.

Alex became a hockey fan when he was only 2 years old. Nothing excited him more than the chance to watch players skating, shooting, and scoring on television. It didn't take long for Alex to decide that he wanted to be a hockey player too.

FAST FACT

As a young hockey fan, Alex Ovechkin's favorite player was Mario Lemieux of the Pittsburgh Penguins. Lemieux was one of the most exciting goal scorers in hockey history. He led the NHL in goals three times. Ovechkin passed his hero by winning the league's goal-scoring title for a fourth time in 2013–14.

Viacheslav Fetisov of the Soviet team during a 1987 tournament in Canada

Sergei Ovechkin, Alex's older brother, introduced a young Alex to the game. By the time he was 8 years old, Alex was enrolled in a sports school in Moscow where he played hockey. When Alex was 10 years old, Sergei died in a car accident. Alex has never forgotten his brother's **influence**. Even today, whenever he scores a goal, he kisses the glove on his left hand and points up in honor of Sergei.

influence—to have an effect on someone or something

AN ATHLETIC FAMILY

Alexander Ovechkin's parents also played sports. His father, Mikhail, was a professional soccer player. His mother, Tatyana, was a superstar just like Alex would become. She played basketball for the Soviet National Team. Tatyana led her country to Olympic gold medals in 1976 and 1980 and a world championship in 1975. She is considered one of the best point guards in the history of Russian women's basketball. Tatyana wore number 8 on her basketball jersey. In honor of his mom, Alex wears number 8 for the Capitals.

Alex trained twice a day at a sports school called Dynamo Moscow. His hard work paid off. He continued to become better at his sport.

By the time he was 16 years old, Alex was a strong, fast hockey player. That year he joined Dynamo's professional hockey team, which was part of the Russian Superleague. He played in just 22 games that first year, scoring two goals and getting two assists. But Alex was on his way to becoming a star.

FAST FACT

The Russian Superleague is now known as the Kontinental Hockey League (KHL). It has 28 teams in eight countries, including 21 teams in Russia. It is considered the second-best hockey league in the world after the NHL.

CHAPTER 3

EVERYONE WANTS ALEX

Still a teenager, Ovechkin quickly was becoming one of the most exciting players in Russia. But he wanted to play against the best players in the world. Those players competed in the United States and Canada in the NHL. Following the breakup of the Soviet Union, many of Russia's best players moved halfway around the world to play in the NHL.

Teams in the NHL wanted Ovechkin to play for them too. They had seen the budding superstar rack up points for Dynamo as well as in **international** competition. During the Under-18 world championship in 2002, the 16-year-old made NHL scouts drool by scoring 14 goals in eight games.

international—including more than one nation

The next year Ovechkin continued to dominate on the world stage. He was named captain of Russia's Under-18 team. He also led the country's Under-20 team to a gold medal at the World Junior Championship, netting two hat tricks in that tournament.

Ovechkin also was asked to play on the Russian men's national team for the first time. He became the youngest player on that **roster**.

roster—a list of players on a team

FAST FACT

Ovechkin has played hockey in the Winter Olympics three times, including in 2014 when it took place in his home country. That year Ovechkin had the honor of being the first Russian athlete to carry the Olympic flame in the torch run from Greece to the Russian city of Sochi.

After his 18th birthday, Ovechkin was old enough to be **drafted** into the NHL. The Washington Capitals had the first pick in the 2004 draft. At least 15 other teams tried to make a trade with Washington so they could draft Ovechkin, but the Capitals wanted him for themselves.

Ovechkin showed fans what was to come during his NHL **debut** October 5, 2005, in Washington, D.C. Playing against the Columbus Blue Jackets, he blasted a slap shot for a goal early in the second period. Less than five minutes later, he scored another goal.

draft—to choose a person to join a sports organization or team

debut—a player's first game

FAST FACT

NHL teams couldn't wait for the chance to draft the talented Ovechkin. The Florida Panthers tried to pick him in 2003 when he was just 17 years old. However, the NHL denied the team's attempt to draft him early.

Ovechkin finished his first season with 52 goals, third most by a rookie in the history of the NHL. He also had 54 assists for 106 **points**, also third most for a rookie.

Scoring 50 goals is a big achievement for an NHL player. During Ovechkin's next eight seasons, he hit that number four more times.

points—a player's total number of goals and assists

ALEX AND SID

Ovechkin and Pittsburgh Penguins star Sidney Crosby have been linked together since they both entered the NHL in 2005. Both were drafted No. 1 overall—Ovechkin in 2004 and Crosby in 2005. A dispute between NHL team owners and players led to the cancellation of the entire 2004–05 season and delayed Ovechkin's debut by a year. Ovechkin and Crosby were both rookies the next season. Ovechkin finished the season with 106 points— four more than Crosby. Ovechkin was named Rookie of the Year. Through nine seasons Ovechkin has 814 points and three Most Valuable Player (MVP) awards but no Stanley Cup rings. Crosby has 769 points, two MVPs, and one championship. The two likely will be compared to each other for the rest of their hockey careers.

CHAPTER 4

OVECHKIN HAS HART

During his third season, 2007–08, Ovechkin became a full-fledged superstar. He earned the nickname "Alexander the GR8," a combination of the name of an ancient king and Ovechkin's jersey number. That year he led the NHL with 65 goals, a total that hadn't been reached in 12 seasons. He also had a league-leading 112 points and won the Hart Trophy as the NHL's most valuable player.

He won the Hart Trophy again the next season after scoring 56 goals and collecting 110 points. It had been 10 seasons since a player won the award in back-to-back seasons. It had been more than 20 years since a forward—Wayne Gretzky—had done it.

Ovechkin was becoming famous. His gap-toothed grin could be seen in television commercials. He appeared on the covers of popular hockey video games, including NHL 07 and NHL 2K10. The Capitals named him team captain midway through the 2009–10 season. That year he scored 50 more goals, and Washington was the best team in the NHL during the regular season.

The NHL played a shortened season due to another disagreement between team owners and players in 2012–13. In 48 games that season, Ovechkin scored 32 goals. He won the Hart Trophy for a third time, something only seven other players—who are all in the **Hall of Fame**—had done before him. The next season Ovechkin once again hit the 50-goal mark, scoring 51 times.

Hall of Fame—a place where people important to the NHL are honored

FAST FACT

Ovechkin moved from left wing to right wing in 2012–13. However, when the NHL's All-Star teams were announced after the season, Ovechkin was honored for playing both positions. He was named first-team right wing and second-team left wing.

Ovechkin had surpassed 400 career goals and 800 points by the end of the 2013–14 season. His statistics and awards have put him on a path to the Hockey Hall of Fame. Just 28 years old at the end of the season, Ovechkin likely has a lot of years left to play and add to his already amazing totals.

QUEST FOR THE CUP

Ovechkin is still waiting for a chance to lift hockey's ultimate prize, the Stanley Cup, over his head. In his first nine seasons, the Capitals went to the playoffs six times. They lost in the first round three times and in the second round three times. In 2009–10 Washington won the Presidents' Trophy, which goes to the team with the best record during the regular season. It looked like the Capitals' year, but the Montreal Canadiens stunned them by beating them in the first round of the playoffs.

One of Ovechkin's trademarks is wearing yellow laces on his skates, but he hardly needs them to stand out from the crowd. For nearly his entire life, he has been one of the most exciting hockey players in the world. His powerful skating, magical hands, and rocket of a shot have frightened opponents and dazzled fans.

From Moscow, the capital of Russia, to Washington, the capital of the United States, he has made people watch in awe whenever he jumps onto the ice. Every time he touches the puck there's a chance to see a spectacular goal—maybe even another one that's worthy of being called "The Goal."

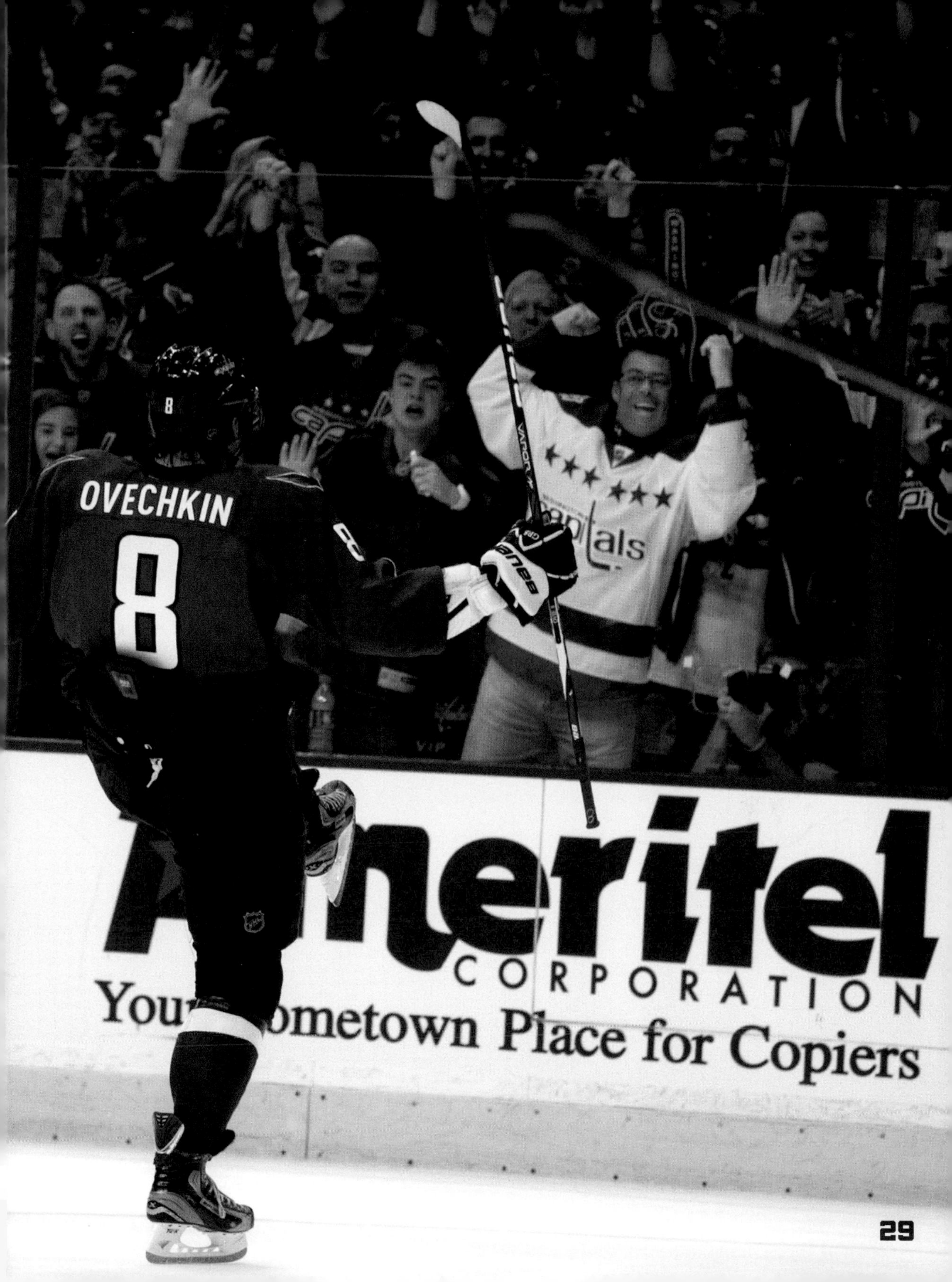
OVECHKIN
8
Capitals
CORPORATION
Place for Copiers

GLOSSARY

debut (DAY-byoo)—a player's first game

defenseman (di-FENS-muhn)—a player who lines up in a defensive zone to prevent opponents from getting open shots on goal

draft (DRAFT)—to choose a person to join a sports organization or team

Hall of Fame (HOL UV FAYM)—a place where people important to the NHL are honored

influence (IN-floo-uhnss)—to have an effect on someone or something

international (in-tur-NASH-uh-nuhl)—including more than one nation

most valuable player (MOHST VAL-yoo-buhl PLAY-ur)—an honor given to the best player each season

points (POYNTZ)—a player's total number of goals and assists

rookie (RUK-ee)—a first-year player

roster (ROSS-tur)—a list of players on a team

Stanley Cup (STAN-lee KUP)—the trophy given each year to the NHL champion

winger (WING-ur)—a type of forward who usually stays near the sides of the zone

READ MORE

Doeden, Matt. *Sidney Crosby: Hockey Superstar.* Sports Illustrated Kids: Superstar Athletes. North Mankato, Minn.: Capstone Press, 2012.

Frederick, Shane. *The Ultimate Collection of Pro Hockey Records.* Sports Illustrated Kids: For the Record. North Mankato, Minn: Capstone Press, 2013.

Jordan, Christopher. *We Are the Goal Scorers: The Top Point Leaders of the NHL.* New York: Fenn/Tundra, 2013.

INTERNET SITES

FactHound offers a safe, fun way to find Internet sites related to this book. All of the sites on FactHound have been researched by our staff.

Here's all you do:

Visit *www.facthound.com*

Type in this code: 9781491421413

Super-cool stuff! Check out projects, games and lots more at www.capstonekids.com

INDEX